WONDER VERSE

Young Creations

First published in Great Britain in 2025 by:

Young Writers
Remus House
Coltsfoot Drive
Peterborough
PE2 9BF
Telephone: 01733 890066
Website: www.youngwriters.co.uk

FOREWORD

WELCOME READER,

For Young Writers' latest competition *Wonderverse*, we asked primary school pupils to explore their creativity and write a poem on any topic that inspired them. They rose to the challenge magnificently with some going even further and writing stories too! The result is this fantastic collection of writing in a variety of styles.

Here at Young Writers our aim is to encourage creativity in children and to inspire a love of the written word, so it's great to get such an amazing response, with some absolutely fantastic pieces. This open theme of this competition allowed them to write freely about something they are interested in, which we know helps to engage kids and get them writing. Within these pages you'll find a variety of topics, from hopes, fears and dreams, to favourite things and worlds of imagination. The result is a collection of brilliant writing that showcases the creativity and writing ability of the next generation.

I'd like to congratulate all the young writers in this anthology, I hope this inspires them to continue with their creative writing.

CONTENTS

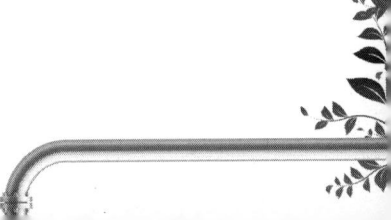

Hawarden Village Church School, Hawarden

Ayla Sezer (8)	56
Zeva Lavender (9)	58
Keira Jones (9)	60
Eleanor Hudson-Young (9)	61
Rhia John (9)	62
Harrison Slade (9)	64
Maya Bubb (9)	65
Mila Edwards (9)	66
Ninah Fenwick (9)	67
Hazel Hodgson (9)	68
Charlie Bellis (9)	69
Caitlin Rate (9)	70
Ted Sefton (9)	71
Albert Hughes (9)	72
Eleanor Dovbenko (9)	73
Theo Edwards (9)	74
Savanna Miotti (9)	75
James Blanchard (9)	76
Theodore Fellows (9)	77
Zach Barnard (9)	78

Holme Slack CP School, Preston

Anamta Malik (9)	79
Tia Rose (8)	80
Lucie Prince (9)	81
Emma Garcia-Castrillon Bejarano (9)	82
Gurmani Kaur (9)	83
Amnah Yusuf (9)	84
Parker Rice (9)	85
Muhammad-Husayn Shah (9)	86
Shehroz Khurram (9)	87
Daniel Mahoney (9)	88
Abdul Rehman (9)	89
Jackson Heap (9)	90

Little Sutton Primary School, Sutton Coldfield

Ben Cooksey (10) & Leo Price (10)	91
Zac Foster (10) & Brian Jin (10)	92
Adam Truby (10)	93
Harvaani Kaur Bassan (10)	94
Isabella Cross (9)	95
Chloe Bugaj (10)	96
Katie Crawford (9)	97
Michael Welch (10)	98

Shotton Primary School, Shotton Colliery

Lucie Ward (10)	99
Jasmine Robson (9)	100
Evelyn Adams (9)	102
Erin Porter (10)	103
Harrison Baker (10)	104
Nathan Thomas Mace (10)	105
Katelyn Bright (10)	106
Isabella Evans (10)	107
Mikey Greener (10)	108

Southwick Primary School, Southwick

Isabella Toms Gascoigne (8)	109
Bella Stead (8)	110
Effy Richardson (8)	111
Oluwakorede Akinola (8)	112
Emmanuella Goodness Osho (8)	113
Anthony Ramon Green Martinez (8)	114
Oluwkitan David Bakare (8)	115
Zoe Oghenovo (8)	116
Lilah June Haddock (8)	118
Nyah-Lee Wright (8)	120
Isaac Huggins (7)	122
Mmasinachi Abasirim (7)	123
Harper Mae Drew Harrison (8)	124
Lilly-Rose Harding	125
Kanzi Hegazi (8)	126
Jenson-James McCririe (8)	127

St Faith's CE Primary School, Wandsworth

Raphaela Papathanasiou (10)	128
Madison McGowan (9)	130
Savino Hoxha (10)	131
Nadia Bigovic (9)	132
Menia Papathanasiou (10)	133
Anna Chornii (10)	134
Cherish Asare (10)	135
Kaleb Mensah (10)	136
Ameiah Stewart (10)	137
Adem De Ruyter (10)	138
Blake Causer (10)	139
Lorelei Hennessy (10)	140
Kiara De Silva (10)	141
Waafi Azim (10)	142
Anthony Do (10)	143
Vanessa Ingabire (9)	144
Bareera Iftiklar (10)	145
Finley Woolford (10)	146
Reuben Balcombe (10)	147

St Thomas' Catholic Primary School, Sevenoaks

Miriam Hunt (11)	148
Mason Vollings (11)	150
Anita Bagchee (10)	152
Alexa Wyss (11)	154
Nina Grahovac (11)	155
Natalia Dziedzic (10)	156
Alessia Ditri (11)	157
Rebecca Henson (11)	158
Nadia Saenz Gonzalez (11)	159
Oscar Grabowski (10)	160
Caroline Tse (11)	161
Anamaria Ford (11)	162
Nikola Wolanin (10)	163
William Durcan (11)	164
Derin Yalman (11)	165
Celestine Disant (11)	166
Andrii Musiyenko (11)	167
Aiyla Longworth (10)	168

Alex Sylvester (11)	169

The Galfrid School, Cambridge

Orlaith Tobin (8)	170
Mariam Amin (8)	171
Leonel Sula (9)	172
Sara Islam (8)	173
Yumi Distura (8)	174
Oliver Dutton (7)	175
Teddy Czlonka (8)	176
Kulsoom Wahid (8)	177
Amy Mukaro (8)	178
Leonardo Pugliese (8)	179
Sophia El Hassani (7)	180

Wayfield Primary School, Chatham

Ava Brown (10)	181
Skylar-Bleu Scott-McKeever (10)	182
Sharon Adetula (10)	184
Molly Banham (9)	186
Lacie Davies (10)	187
Yensi Kwalar (9)	188
Oreoluwa Ajayi (8)	190
Darcey Thomas (10)	191
Daisy Eldridge (9)	192
Summer Passcall (10)	193
Louise Robertson (8)	194
Sadie Rae Stevens (10)	195
Teddie Lycett (8)	196
Poppy Yeates (10)	197
Melody Ovbigbaghon (9)	198
Iona Patrick-Ononye (8)	199
Darcy Fuller (8)	200
Deekshitha Dhibin (8)	201
Poppy Groves (9)	202
Teddie Beaumont (9)	203
Gorav Adit Donthuiapoina (8)	204

THE CREATIVE WRITING

The Stress Of Being A Cat Owner

The cat is a cute, unique creature
But that one time at night
They are quite a fright...
Because they snatch your bed
Scratch your head
And wake you up from quite a good sleep
Just for food, and that puts you in a mood!
Groaning, moaning, crying, yawning
Is what really happens when they sit next to their
dinner bowl!
Hissing, growling, nothing new!
Just watch the fight and eat your stew!
Your cat, my cat! All the same
They only have a different name!
If you're lucky enough
They might bring you a surprise!
Mice or birds? You decide!
It all depends if they think you're nice
Then the day resets...
The same, same, again... and again... and again.

Cleo Cosgrove (10)
Cedars Primary School, Newport Pagnell

Read More

Nestle under the starlit sky
Let the fireworks fly
Let the stars all cry
For in this space
It's an endless race
What shall I read today?

Nestle under your warm, fluffy coat
Imagine yourself in Ratty's blue boat
Watch Charlie and Grandpa weightlessly float
Because when you read
The stories will bleed
And set in an unforgettable way.

Nestle down for a well-deserved nap
Meet a wizard called Harry (a very nice chap)
See a tall, grey cat with his new red cap
Engulf the pages one by one
Soon you'll find your imagination spun
Into a crisscross of wonderful things
It will be so full, we will all feel like kings
But if you want to enchant your core
My only message is to *read more!*

Annabelle Hackett (11)
Cedars Primary School, Newport Pagnell

Green Winning Machine

Upon the 3G pitch I stand
With nervous energy and sweaty hands.
The whistle blows, the game begins.
The ball is passed straight to the wing.
We run up front, their goal in sight.
The keeper dives left, the shot goes right.

The game is competitive, parents are cheering.
Crunching tackles as half-time is nearing.
The crowd lets out a deafening roar
As we put the ball in the net once more.

Half-time has come, and confidence is strong.
With more effort to give, the break isn't too long.
Back on the pitch, and everything clicks.
The team is electric, and passes are quick.

Our faces are a rosy red
And sweat is dripping from our heads
But the tide is constant, green and fast.
Another, another, and finally a last!

The final whistle blows today.
Five-nil to the Swans!
Hip hip hooray!

Erin Wilkie (10)
Cedars Primary School, Newport Pagnell

The Teacher Anthem

What do teachers say every day, well...
One, two, three, all eyes on me,
Where is the missing glue stick lid?
The bell doesn't dismiss you, I dismiss you.
It's your time you're wasting, Year Eight,
Stop swinging on your chair, Gary.
Why do I hear talking?
You must wear your blazers, it's only forty degrees
outside.
Just put a wet paper towel on it,
Remember to show your working out, I'll wait.
You had a break three hours ago, you should've gone
then.
Uh, Year Nines, don't kick my basketballs,
We are not Year Five anymore, this is Year Six,
So, can we start acting like it?
Year Sevens, you have your GCSEs in five years,
So, can you turn the volume down?
We are in maths, not art,
So, can we stop drawing fancy 'S's on the whiteboard?
You have only had your whiteboard pens for nine
months,
Why are they running out?
Can I go to the toilet? It's *may* I go to the toilet!

Sara Lamanna-Amieva (11)
Cedars Primary School, Newport Pagnell

Every Ending Is A New Beginning

Today I lay on grass so wide, with sunshine shining on my side,
And thought my thoughts combined, one tiny thought just couldn't get out of my mind.
Later I had that terrifying feeling, but then it went from my shore of thoughts... As it was gone it left a tinge of questions too.
The question sounded so simple, yet the answer was so hard, so
"Does something happen when we die?"
Well, you can assume the response, for hours, days or years,
But there's one thing I know for sure,
Every ending is a new beginning.
That's why we don't need to worry about the turning of pages in the book of life.
Love the life, because our love lives on! Our love lives on!

Anna Kuzmych (11)
Cedars Primary School, Newport Pagnell

Don't Be Afraid To Fall

Don't be afraid to fall,
Even if you get bucked off into a wall.
Remember, no time is wasted in the saddle,
So if you are in deep water,
Use them as a paddle,

Don't be afraid if you get kicked in the head,
Even if you end up in a hospital bed.
Remember, if they slow you down, don't frown,
Because they have bad days too.
So, give them a scratch, rub their itchy patch,
And tickle under their chin, coochy coo.

Don't be afraid, they feel your feelings,
Even if they stand around squealing.
Remember, you love them
And they love you,
It's a bond that won't break soon.
So don't be afraid to fall.

Suri Geldart (11)
Cedars Primary School, Newport Pagnell

Scary Frights And TV Nights

I watched a scary movie last night
It gave me quite a fright
I got scared and needed a light
Even though my eyes were shut tight.

Scary thoughts were in my head
I thought there were monsters under my bed
Mum couldn't help, no matter what she said
I still saw ghosts and the walking dead.

Every time I closed my eyes
I got a horrible surprise
I could still hear the creatures' cries
And see the rotting zombies rise.

I watched a funny show yesterday
It took my fears and worries away
My head was filled with laughter and play
"Don't watch horrors," my mum would say!

Taylor Lockley (11)
Cedars Primary School, Newport Pagnell

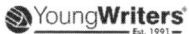
My Class Pet

We have a class pet, he lives under the teacher's desk.
Our class pet is very quiet, can you guess what it is?
We have a class pet, he lives under the teacher's desk.
He is very quiet, he is very small.
Can you guess what it is?
We have a class pet, he lives under the teacher's desk.
He is very quiet, he is very small.
Our teacher does not know what it is.
Can you guess what it is?
We have a class pet, he lives under the teacher's desk.
He is very quiet, he is very small.
Our teacher does not know about him.
He is an ant! Did you know that?

Anna Watts (10)
Cedars Primary School, Newport Pagnell

The Looking Glass

I looked inside the looking glass, what wonders might I
see?
Everything in there was looking back at me.
I stepped inside, and a small rabbit said, "Hi!"
"Oh, hello little rabbit," I said, with a start.
I glanced behind my shoulder, no looking glass in sight!
I asked if the rabbit saw one with a fright
"There are none in these parts," he said, "They were in
a mountain way up high."
"That's far up?" I said with a sigh.
"You have to be joking! If I climb that,
I'll fall down with a splat!"

Annabelle Brindle Hall (9)
Cedars Primary School, Newport Pagnell

The Emotional Ball Of Wool

Feelings are like a ball of wool,
You don't always know what's what.
Sometimes they get tangled up and make you feel a lot!
Happy, worried, sad and mad,
They can be overwhelming and big.
It's like a crazy dance inside your head,
A messy, jumbled jig.

When it feels like this,
You might need help to untangle.
You could talk to a friend, write it down,
Have a hug to see it from a different angle.
So when your wool is muddled up or in a fiddly knot,
Use these tools to pull the wool,
They can help a lot!

Edie Avann (10)
Cedars Primary School, Newport Pagnell

Roses And Violets Are Beautiful, But You Are Too!

Roses are red,
Violets are blue,
But why aren't there other flowers,
Included too?
Lilies are delicately light,
Although sunflowers,
Are awfully bright.

As spring comes close soon,
Nature begins to bloom.
Tulips,
Whilst forgotten,
Are captivatingly colourful,
Just like irises,
Oh, so marvellously wonderful.

Everyone is perfect,
Just the way they are.
Never lose hope,
Because you're a superstar.

Rose Connolly (11)
Cedars Primary School, Newport Pagnell

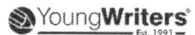

The Joy Of Dance

The best feeling ever comes right away
From putting on the outfit to feeling yourself sway.

No one can judge with the joy of dance.

We dance to express, not to impress
Your jaw will ache after from all of the laughter.

No one can judge with the joy of dance.

And the best bit of all is when
You walk up proudly to do your exam.

No one can judge with the joy of dance.
No one can judge with the joy of dance.

Lucy Watts (10)
Cedars Primary School, Newport Pagnell

I'm Not A Stick

I'm not a stick
I'm a pogo stick
I'm an umbrella
I'm not a stick
I'm a pull-up bar
I'm a river
I'm not a stick
I'm a footscratcher as well as a backscratcher
I'm not a stick pencil
As I say, I'm not a stick, I'm a pole
I'm a table leg
I'm not a stick
I'm a washing line,
I'm a straw
I'm not a stick.

Marcelo Vaz (10)
Cedars Primary School, Newport Pagnell

The Wild

W acky and authentic
I n different landscapes and habitats
L urking in jungles
D aring to be wild

W herever they could hide
O minous beings from the sky to the ocean
N o one dares to hunt them
D oes anyone care about their home?
E verywhere is being destroyed
R escue the animals
S o stop deforestation.

Sydney Lee (9)
Cedars Primary School, Newport Pagnell

Things You Can Do With A Leaf

There are many things you can do with a leaf
A blanket for a mouse
A roof for a house
A rug for a room
The bristles of a broom
A replacement for a mat
A cape for a cat
A duvet for a beetle
The cap for a steeple
A napkin for a dog
A disguise for a frog
A cotton wool pad
The only thing that makes your dad mad.

Evelyn Briceanu (11)
Cedars Primary School, Newport Pagnell

Pizza Topping

What would Mona Lisa like on her pizza?
Does she have a favourite topping?
Now I fancy pizza, I'd better go shopping.
Pepperoni pizza is in the oven.
Soon, I will be in heaven.
1st slice, 2nd slice, 3rd slice,
Then a drink of Diet Coke with ice.
4th slice, 5th slice, 6th slice.
Wow, my favourite pizza was nice.

Alfie Anderson (11)
Cedars Primary School, Newport Pagnell

The Manic, Magic Space Effect

The manic, magic space effect,
It is an emotion that can't be grown,
It's an overload of anger and fear,
It is planted deep in each and every soul.
It was made by Tim, Tim Glarty,
Manic from head to toe.
He was in space, and when he came down,
He went mad at his magically deformed leg bones.

Eli Cessford-Row (10)
Cedars Primary School, Newport Pagnell

Fire Lions

In a jungle not too far away,
The fire lions come to play.

Their manes glow like a flame,
Surely, their names are not lame.

They roar so loud,
It can even move a cloud.

If you see a glow in the night,
It could be a lion shining bright.

Caleb Sushil (8)
Cedars Primary School, Newport Pagnell

What Is Friendship?

Friendship is
With a miss
That you feel
She's your sis.
Friendship grows
Like vines on trees
Moving on
Like a song.
Some friendships can get you low

So...
Be careful with who you be
Don't get in trouble just like me.

Lena Poszwa (10)
Cedars Primary School, Newport Pagnell

A Little Mouse

I'm a little mouse and I live in a house,
And my name is Bryce and I'm very nice.
My favourite thing to do is jump,
Even over a big hump.
I have a friend called Ted,
And his dad's name is Ed.
I like to eat worms,
Even if they squirm.

Rowan Taylor (8)
Cedars Primary School, Newport Pagnell

Cheesecake

I like cheesecake, cheesecake likes me,
Everybody likes it, and you like it too,
Everybody eats it, yum, yum, yum,
And the cheesecake says, "Hi,"
And you say, "Oh my god,"
And then you say, "Hi."

Gracie Collins (7)
Cedars Primary School, Newport Pagnell

The Land Shark

Deep under the hot, hot sand
It lay softly, until...
The sound closed in.
The land shark went to the hot sand
The land shark burned itself
But in the wind, some sneakers fell.
He went to the hot sand and put them on.

Harley Lane (9)
Cedars Primary School, Newport Pagnell

Fire

Fire, fire burning bright
What a lovely sight tonight
Ashes, ashes that look like dashes
The flames rising
Moon is flying
The smoke makes me choke
The light that takes flight.

Mac Ainscow (11)
Cedars Primary School, Newport Pagnell

Me

I am me
I am who I want to be
I love me
I don't care what people think about me
I am proud of me
I love who I am
I am me!

Georgia Rowlands (11)
Cedars Primary School, Newport Pagnell

Kitty Run

Kitty, kitty, run, just run
People are chasing you
And you're scared
So run
Oh, kitty, kitty run.

Alexander Ajit Singh Lagah (7)
Cedars Primary School, Newport Pagnell

A Cherry Tree Grows

A seed is planted deep in the damp, dark dirt.
The ground quakes, and a crack shatters the soil's silence.
A cherry tree starts to grow!
Tiny roots wriggle, breaking free from their motherly shell.
The sun and rushing rain work together,
Nurturing the tree with gentle care.
A cherry tree is growing!
A stalk breaks free, strong and fearless,
Facing stormy, hot and freezing seasons.
A cherry tree grows!
After years of reaching and rustling,
Losing rosy-pink petals that flutter to the ground like snowflakes.
Covering the emerald grass below.
A cherry tree stands tall!
With a whisper of wind, a gift of time,
A deep-brown seed drops gently from its graceful mother.
A cherry tree starts to grow.

Shannon Daley (10)
Etching Hill Primary Academy, Rugeley

Friendship's The Best

My friends are the best,
They always help me when I need it,
If I didn't have my friends, I don't know what I'd do.

Maybe I'd be bored, with nobody to play with,
There wouldn't be much laughing, as who would get
my joke?
Football would be rubbish with nobody in goal,
Water fights would be pointless, as who would be there
to soak?

I'll always have good friends, but some stand out,
Whenever I need help, they'll always be about.
Sometimes in football when I've been feeling down,
They've put their arms around me and told me not to
frown.

Friendship is special, as it fills my life with joy,
And to the person reading this, I hope you also have a
friend to enjoy!

Harper Boate (10)
Etching Hill Primary Academy, Rugeley

My Letter To The Future

A letter to my future me, a letter to future me.
Do I have a dog? A job? A little family.
Am I a good person? Are people proud of me?

Do we still bite our nails and pick our noses?
Do we still love trainers, because at the moment I have loads.
Does Dad still have a beard? Is Mum's hair still long?
Do we still love music? What's our new favourite song?

How's Nan's knees? Does she still need a stick?
Does she still walk slowly, or can she run really quick?
I hope I did good so that you're doing better.
I'm only ten, writing future me this letter.

Reggie Carter (10)
Etching Hill Primary Academy, Rugeley

Each Year

Each year is very long,
Four seasons it will be,
Each is different from the rest,
Then we start all over again.

Winter is wet and cold,
It's hard to stay dry and warm.
The darkness comes early every day,
Dreaming of the warmer days.

Spring is full of what will be,
The promise of food to come.
Life starts to blossom,
New life is on its way.

Summer is when you're touched by the sun,
Every day is a blessing.
Food is growing in the fields,
What a happy time to be alive.

Abel Beaman (9)
Etching Hill Primary Academy, Rugeley

Why Did I Grow Up?

The world I knew, a playground free now, has a
different hue,
Growing up, I learnt the truth, though it's hard and
new.
A moment's pause, a breath held tight,
Before embracing day and night.
Take it back? Well, I wish I could,
Back to a time when life seemed good.
And they wonder why we lie, cheat and steal,
Well, they never prepared us for a world so unreal.
As time unfolds,
My happiness falls.
What once was a dream,
Became a scheme.
Even when I'm low,
I still know I have my family and co.

Evaline Labuschange (10)
Etching Hill Primary Academy, Rugeley

Space Pioneer

S pace is an eternity of dark,

P ioneering leaves its mark.

A dventuring into darkness.

C reating the image of a black mess.

E ventually creating a sense of fear.

P rinting the image of something near.

I magining a creature lurking around.

O nly hiding under a scary mound.

N ever let anyone in.

E ventually they will stab you in the back with a pin.

E ternity is a long time.

w **R** ens are sitting in a pine.

Alfie Maxfield (9)

Etching Hill Primary Academy, Rugeley

Brazil

Clear skies,
Up in the air.
Sun in my eyes,
Wind in my hair.

Listen to the toucans sing,
Watch the waves crash on the shore,
While I hear the music ring,
And the fish bite your lure.

With my cousins in the pool,
And also swimming in the lake.
Six weeks' holiday away from school,
All I eat is beans, rice and steak.

Everyone is having fun,
No one is ever stressed.
All I do is play and run,
That's why summer is the best.

Olivia Powell (10)
Etching Hill Primary Academy, Rugeley

The Magic Of The Ocean

The ocean's a blanket,
Of sparkly fun,
With fish that zoom,
Under the baking sun.
A turtle's shell is a bungalow,
A place to live,
A place to grow.

The coral is candy,
In bubblegum-pink,
While sneaky squids,
Squirt smoky black ink.

The ocean has a thumping heart,
That beats with magic,
Wild and smart.
It hides some secrets,
It hides some dreams,
And shines with sunlight's golden beams.

Lily Spires (10)
Etching Hill Primary Academy, Rugeley

My Sister And Me

One of three,
My sisters and me,
They may be older,
But I'm up to their shoulders.

They make a mess,
And like fancy dress,
They stain the floor,
With makeup and all.

They take long baths,
But at least they make me laugh,
We go for walks,
And have long talks.

One of three,
My sisters and me,
I may be the only boy,
But they still bring me joy.

Aquilus Boyer Rankine (10)
Etching Hill Primary Academy, Rugeley

The Sunny Beach

The sun shines bright,
The sand is warm,
Little waves crash,
Gentle storm,
Seashells scattered,
Like untold treasures,
Tiny feet running,
Brave and bold.

Buckets and shovels,
Castles arise in glistening sands,
Reflecting the skies,
Seagulls are soaring,
With joyful sounds,
Happy echoes all around.

Scarlett Penillim (10)
Etching Hill Primary Academy, Rugeley

Fish And Sticks

At the top of the stairs, sat four glass walls
With water filled to the top.
Inside were little orange blobs floating about.
Rocks stacked high like a mountain.
Every day, a storm of flakes was unleashed.
Bluebell pebbles littered around.
Scales shimmered.
Tiny mirrors.
Marble-like eyes searching for each other.

Arthur Upton (10)
Etching Hill Primary Academy, Rugeley

Ernest Shackleton

Ernest Shackleton was an intrepid explorer. Shackleton was stuck on an elephant island for more than 300 days. Shackleton's crew were a very good crew, because he had a chef, doctors, and everything you could name.
Suddenly, disaster struck. The Endurance boat was stuck in solid ice, like an almond in the middle of a chocolate.

Calum Mcausland (9)
Etching Hill Primary Academy, Rugeley

Friendship

F riends forever
R emembering birthdays
I nside-out knowledge of them
E qual
N ever lies
D on't be nasty!
S ticking together
H elping when needed
I nvolved in their problems
P rotecting each other.

Meadow Price (10)
Etching Hill Primary Academy, Rugeley

Spain

S panish weather is so nice, like I'm in paradise

P laying in the sea, feeling free

A lways in the water, the weather getting hotter and hotter

I n the sun all day, even though it's only May

N ever want to come back, but I have to keep on track!

Isabella Adesina (10)

Etching Hill Primary Academy, Rugeley

Seasons

S unny days and raining, to
E ach one brings something new
A utumn leaves fall to the ground
S now in the winter falls all around
O pen flowers in spring
N ew things grow and birds sing
S ummer's fun is here to stay.

Joey Ensor (10)
Etching Hill Primary Academy, Rugeley

All About Space

S pace has eight planets

P luto is a dwarf planet, one of five

A cross the galaxy there are millions of stars

C reated and destroyed every day

E verything in space holds a purpose, we are just one part.

Dougie Kitchener (9)

Etching Hill Primary Academy, Rugeley

Snowman

I built a snowman,
He had an orange nose,
A warm coat,
Fun to build,
But the fun had to end.
And when it's winter,
I'll build it again.

Barney Bullock (9)
Etching Hill Primary Academy, Rugeley

Our Wonder World

There are eight planets in our solar system,
If you know them all, you're full of wisdom,
The moon glows only at night,
So that it doesn't give the sun a fright,
Mars and Uranus, to name a few,
Neptune and Saturn join the queue,
Pluto and Venus are another two,
The Milky Way comes into play,
And all are here to stay,
Without them all, the Earth would not exist,
And all would turn into mist,
So give all our planets a mighty cheer,
When we look through the telescope at our wondrous
atmosphere,
Now all of us on Earth can live without fear.

Charlotte Hibberd (8)
Farmborough Church Primary School, Farmborough

Chocolate Cake

Chocolate cake is all I like,
If I have anything else, it gives me a fright,
I have it day after day,
Nothing can keep me away,
Sometimes I bring it to school,
I would even have it in the pool,
Sometimes, it makes me drool,
If I have too much, it will turn me into a fool,
If you don't like it, you're uncool,
It makes me want to play with a ball,
It makes me really playful,
I think I could look after a bull,
I could sew ten times faster with wool,
Even better on a stool,
Chocolate cake is the best,
My brother has bad numbers on his test,
I am a little pest,
I am really stressed,
I even get pressed,
My chocolate cake is blessed,
I keep it to my chest,
Sometimes, I give it to a guest,
I would put crumbs in the bird's nest,

It is so good,
I brought it to the woods,
It is lovely food,
It makes me feel better if I'm in a mood,
It would never be in a stew,
Chocolate cake is the best!

Poppy Bartholomew (8)

Farmborough Church Primary School, Farmborough

My Favourite Animal

In the plains of Africa, there is movement in the grass.
My favourite animal is powerful and fast.
Slowly and deliberately, she creeps up on her prey.
This will be over quickly, in an awesome display.
The antelope were grouped together in a bunch
With no idea one of them is lunch.
The cheetah then decides to run,
For one of the poor deer, its time is done.
By the time the group saw her it was already too late
Because when cheetah is charging, it's a certain fate.
A swipe of the paw and in for the kill,
Cheetah has won and antelope is a meal.

Hannah Lippiatt (8)
Farmborough Church Primary School, Farmborough

Supercross

Motocross is a fun sport
You could do it rain or shine
Maybe you're too tall or too short
But that trophy will be mine

Big, knobbly tyres dig into the dirt
Sometimes you might get hurt
But you will always mend
And come out on top at the end

The feel of the bike as you enter the bend
Lean left and right, may the track never end

The feel of wind while soaring through the air
Could never compare
To the feeling of adrenaline pulsing
Through the veins, or the sound of the chain.

Reggie Prowse (8)
Farmborough Church Primary School, Farmborough

BOTW

Breath of the Wild is a single-player game.
If you go in, you won't come out the same.

Your name is Link
The chosen knight
With you in control
You will win every fight

You are trying to save Zelda from dying alone,
She uses her powers to protect her home

With King Rhoam Bosphoramus
And the NPC Thomas,
You're shown the way
Whenever you play

Holding back Ganon's scattered attacks
She never gives up, and you've got her back!

Finley Whipp (7)
Farmborough Church Primary School, Farmborough

Camping By The Sea

Our camping holiday, it's here at last!
The excitement now feels really vast.
I simply cannot wait to play,
Every minute of every day.
Making friends in the park,
Playing football 'til it's dark.
Board games, we're back again,
Best to five... or maybe ten.
Tired from fresh air,
Sandy feet washed and salty hair.
All hungry tummies fed,
Tucked up in bed.
There is nowhere else I would like to be,
Than with my family by the sea.

Ewan Mcillivemon (7)
Farmborough Church Primary School, Farmborough

Gymnastics

I love gymnastics, it is really good fun.
Maybe you should come along.
We practise different skills,
Like jumps, rolls and twirls.

We do floor, bars, beam, vault and flips,
With a wiggle of our hips.
My favourite skills are backend kickovers,
Handstands and round-offs.

What will you choose?
I have earned medals, you can too!
Go on, give it a try,
Don't be shy!

Dora Escott (8)
Farmborough Church Primary School, Farmborough

School

School is really boring,
I just can't stop yawning.
The teacher tells us what to do,
Every single morning.

Break is really fun,
Because we can play in the sun,
And run around with our friends,
Until break is done.

I suppose I shouldn't whine,
I sometimes have a good time.
If I didn't go to school,
I wouldn't be able to write this rhyme.

Trudence Jenkins Moore (8)
Farmborough Church Primary School, Farmborough

Minecraft

Minecraft is a game,
I love it, it's not lame.
My name is Steve,
Play quickly before I leave.

Look out! There's a chicken jockey,
Run up that hill, even if it's rocky.

There was an explosion from a creeper.
Hurry up, and dig down deeper.

Malaki Herren (9)
Farmborough Church Primary School, Farmborough

The Squirrel

On a very sunny day
A baby squirrel came into my garden.
It was as small as a mouse
And I think it had lost its way.

I gave it some nuts and some water to drink
I left it alone for some time to think.
When I returned, it had gone
I hope it found its mum.

Jude Thompson (8)
Farmborough Church Primary School, Farmborough

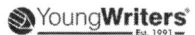

Who-O-Saurus?

He lived around 100 million years ago,
In a world full of dinos,
He waits to ambush his prey,
A giant fish swims by,
With a flash of his teeth,
He grabs it,
His favourite food to gobble up,
This is a spinosaurus.

Lewys Edwards (7)
Farmborough Church Primary School, Farmborough

Space

S pace
P luto
A stronaut
C omet
E arth

E arth
A pollo
R ocket
T itan
H ubble telescope.

Ralphy Murray (8)
Farmborough Church Primary School, Farmborough

Life As A Royal Corgi

Ah, life as a royal corgi is such a delight!
I love standing on the royal balcony
Dancing and, of course, barking!
Sneaking onto the King's throne
And my dear posing on it.
Getting my hair brushed at the parlours:
Ooh, what a treat!
And dancing in the street.

But sometimes it's really hard
Because the King says I can only have one law a year
I can choose to keep the one I have
Or change it to a different law. Uh...
But the good thing is I'm royalty.

So yeah, my bedroom is the best
With gold carat everything!
My bed is as soft as a rabbit
And as squishy as a sponge.
My dog food is human food.
I know I'm spoiled.

I love, love, love going to the pet shop
I get to spend millions of pounds - yippee!
Sometimes I get to sit on the Queen's lap
When she's going in the car.
I just have to say:
You need to morph into a royal corgi!

Ayla Sezer (8)
Hawarden Village Church School, Hawarden

Tudors

Henry VIII was a cruel old fellow,
In fact, his teeth were a little bit yellow.
He also hated his six wives,
He was anything but nice.

His children, Lizzie, Eddie and Mary,
You might think they were kinder,
But they were just more precise.

Young Eddie ruled at nine,
Elegant Eddie did school,
But in the castle's rules,
He soon died at fifteen,
He never even got a queen.

Then soon along came mad Mary,
She was as mean as a pixie,
Even she was a little bit tricky,
She burned over 300 protestants,
And gave the Catholic the Pope.

Then there was Mary's sister Elizabeth,
You would not want to cross her,
So much like her father,
Eating and everything, even chopping off heads,
Had sugarlumps from a bowl,
Made her teeth go golden.

Zeva Lavender (9)
Hawarden Village Church School, Hawarden

I Wish

The castle is as old as time,
Standing proud in the sun that shines.
Crown Jewels gleam and glow,
The moat's water flows and flows.
Sitting on my throne gave me a bore,
So I decided to run away, or...
Be as brave as a knight,
Be as dark as night,
Listen to the chirping birds in the morning sunlight!

Oh how I wish, I wish to do all this,
But all I get to do is sit.
The king was as sly as a fox,
"Heads up!" he called to the servant walking past,
It broke as it was really old.
Uh-oh, what was I thinking?!
I guess I'll hide it in the kitchen... or...
Maybe in my bedroom where no one would see, or, hang on,
I can't think of any more...
Never mind, I'll stick to queen,
But the royal life is pretty mean.

Keira Jones (9)
Hawarden Village Church School, Hawarden

The King's Knights

The king's knights, fierce and bold,
Ready for battle, ready for gold,
Attacking soldiers and climbing boulders,
Killing queens and killing kings,
We're the winners - watch us sing.

The king's knights, hungry as bulls,
Eat and eat until full,
Beer or wine to drink for me,
More meat, and for me!

The king's knights zoom in to protect,
Horses trot around the castle,
The enemy, strong and dangerous,
But we're the wealthy winners once and for all!

The king's knights, old as history,
We're them, the king's knights,
We're in the past, strong and bold,
We'll live there till we're old!

Eleanor Hudson-Young (9)
Hawarden Village Church School, Hawarden

Life As A Royal

People think that being royal,
Would be very nice,
But for me,
The rules are really tight.
I have to wear ballgowns,
All the time.
But all I really want,
Is to be a knight.
It's always,
"Get on that balcony!"
Or, "Wave, be polite!"
Do this, do that,
Hey, I don't remember that cat.

So I asked Dad for some armour,
But obviously he said no.
So I snuck out at night,
Went to the knight test,
And guess what?
I passed!

So maybe life as a royal,
Isn't that bad.
Okay, I was wrong,
I'm queen in ten minutes.
Dad, please come back!
But I stopped and thought,
What Dad had said.
Okay, I'll be a knight instead.

Rhia John (9)
Hawarden Village Church School, Hawarden

Life As A King

Life as a king is like being the ruler of the world,
because you live in an amazing castle.
A butler who does whatever you want.
You get to make life-changing decisions
You get to sit on a majestic, dazzling, glimmering
throne
You get to eat whatever you want, and you can be
strong like a man in battle
The castle that you live in stands proudly in the
sunshine.

A battle takes place outside the castle
Let's make sure there is no hassle.
You get to wear a beautiful, shiny crown
Life as a king is amazing, and that's why
Life as a king is so nice, but make sure you do it right.

Harrison Slade (9)
Hawarden Village Church School, Hawarden

Tudor Times

T he rotten Tudor times come back to life,

U gly kings and queens torture their pupils,

D ie or live, you won't survive with them,

O ccupied, getting ready to fight, *bang, bang!*

R ubbish meat the king would eat, but all the poor ate was vegetables.

T empers the Tudors had if they didn't get what they wanted,

I ncidents happened every day because of them,

M ean, head-chopping King Henry VIII and Elizabeth loved it,

E very day, violence is shown,

S mile not, unless you want to get your head chopped off!

Maya Bubb (9)

Hawarden Village Church School, Hawarden

Royal Corgis

C orgis are cute and colourful,
O verflowingly hungry and over-excited,
R oyal and riot,
G nashing eaters and great cuddlers,
I ndistinguishable breed, and independent,
S urprising and super.

A re adorable and amazing,
R eally fluffy and really fun,
E nergetic and everything cute.

R eigning and respectful,
O minous and old breed,
Y appy and yellow crown,
A lmighty and adorable,
L oving and loyal.

Mila Edwards (9)
Hawarden Village Church School, Hawarden

Executing Glories

B oleyn and Howard (Henry's wives) got beheaded because they betrayed horrid Henry.

E veryone hates the guillotine, they know what it means!

H enry VIII loved to chop his wives' heads off. Don't marry him!

E xecuting was very popular in the Tudor times.

A nne Boleyn got beheaded because she cheated with five people.

D eath is on the way when you hear that slash.

E very peasant keeps out of trouble.

D on't go near the axe.

Ninah Fenwick (9)

Hawarden Village Church School, Hawarden

Kings And Queens Of Time

T he kings' and queens' reign of power, good children
roam the town to the anger of their parents

H e killed and married and killed, but he got six wives
and three children

R oom is covered in gold and bronze on the crown;
however king and queen rage over it

O n the crown, it glows with brightness from silver to
rubies to emeralds to diamonds

N ow in royal King Charles III

E mperors and kings are the same thing.

Hazel Hodgson (9)

Hawarden Village Church School, Hawarden

Executioner Poem

E xcellent at head chopping,

X marks the spot where the head falls,

E xtremely scary,

C rash the blood goes,

U gly man covered in blood,

T oo many people have died,

I am glad they are gone,

"**O** h no, he's coming," they said,

N obody dares to be bad,

E verybody knows about him,

R eally should not have been a thing.

Charlie Bellis (9)

Hawarden Village Church School, Hawarden

The Royal Riddle

They rule the country,
They are as old as time,
They wave till their hands hurt,
They will always be remembered,
They make all the decisions,
They have a crown to themselves,
They go down in history,
They wear fur on themselves,
People learn about them,
They are very important,
What are they?

Answer: A king!

Caitlin Rate (9)
Hawarden Village Church School, Hawarden

Heavy Lies The Crown

C rafty crown makes people know that you are a king or queen,

R uby-red shiny gems carved into the crown,

O ff with the head, the king is dead, the crown gets a new owner,

W ith lots of kings dead, the crown still stands with a new king who likes to execute,

N othing stands a chance with the crown's pointy head.

Ted Sefton (9)

Hawarden Village Church School, Hawarden

Castle Poem

C olossal building the size of lots of houses inside and out.

A ttractive people, old and young, live here as the world walks on by.

S tunning history in its past.

T owers in its heights as tall as can be.

L ots of water around the outside.

E very king and queen lived in one of these.

Albert Hughes (9)

Hawarden Village Church School, Hawarden

The Monarch's Throne

T o go to battle, my users shall change,

H ow long will my glory shine on?

R age will engulf my owners when war is set,

O ne chance I have to survive,

N o one will praise me - only monarchs get it,

E veryone wishes to sit on my cushion, not because of me, only the power I come with.

Eleanor Dovbenko (9)

Hawarden Village Church School, Hawarden

The Royal Sense Poem

I can see a cracking castle falling into crumbles.
I can smell the blood of knights who fought in battle.
I can touch the silk of the king's throne.
I can hear the king, stomping down the hall.
I can taste royalty around the whole place.

Theo Edwards (9)
Hawarden Village Church School, Hawarden

Royalty

R ude to interrupt the royals,

O ld history, old crown,

Y ears of battles, years and times,

A cross time so long,

L aunching luck around life,

T eam royalty,

Y ears so long ago.

Savanna Miotti (9)

Hawarden Village Church School, Hawarden

A Tudor Tale

K nights line up in shining armour.
I n the castle, the Crown Jewels lie.
N aughty children fill the streets.
G ood kings and queens.
S miley king parades around the street.

James Blanchard (9)
Hawarden Village Church School, Hawarden

Kings

K ings are royal.

I think kings are good.

N obody thinks the king is bad.

G o and see the king at the castle.

S mile at the king when you see him.

Theodore Fellows (9)

Hawarden Village Church School, Hawarden

Untitled

K illing king
I ncredibly big
N ice queens rule the UK.
G reat kings and queens
S hining crowns on their heads.

Zach Barnard (9)
Hawarden Village Church School, Hawarden

Untitled

I'm fifteen years old.
I don't like learning.
I don't like going to school, it's boring.
I act like I'm sick.

I'm twenty years old.
I am so modern.
I like going outside to play.
I like to play football.

I'm sixty years old.
I don't remember anything.
My children are older now.
I always hurt my back.

Anamta Malik (9)
Holme Slack CP School, Preston

Untitled

I am thirty years old.
I am very well married.
I have really, really bad diarrhoea.
I have armpit hair.

I'm one hundred years old.
My back hurts a lot.
I will die very, very, very soon.
I like to sit down.

I'm thirteen years old.
High school is very hard.
I work very, very hard at school.
I am a hard worker.

Tia Rose (8)
Holme Slack CP School, Preston

Untitled

I am eleven years old
High school sounds boring.
I will miss my friends.
I don't want to go to high school.

I am eighty years old.
I'm as old as a mountain.
Today is my birthday.

I am one hundred years old.
I am as old as a rock.
One hundred is too old, okay.

Lucie Prince (9)
Holme Slack CP School, Preston

Untitled

I'm thirteen years old
I just started high school
Next year is college

I'm twenty years old
I am studying hard
I am nearly grown up
I'm so tired now

I'm sixty years old
I am nearly retired
I am in a nursing home
I now wear glasses.

Emma Garcia-Castrillon Bejarano (9)
Holme Slack CP School, Preston

Untitled

I'm twelve years old.
I don't want to go to school.
I will miss my friends.

I'm twenty years old.
When I'm twenty, my back hurts.
I will sleep a lot.

I'm sixty years old.
When I am sixty, I will be tired.
I will nap a lot.

Gurmani Kaur (9)
Holme Slack CP School, Preston

Untitled

Haiku poetry

I'm thirteen years old
Dad already bought the milk
My mum bought it, too.

I'm twenty years old
My grandma takes care of me
And now I've left her.

I'm forty years old
I have got a house right now
And I broke my back.

Amnah Yusuf (9)
Holme Slack CP School, Preston

Untitled

Haiku poetry

I'm twenty years old.
College is too stressful now.
I am so lonely.

I'm sixty years old.
What is this generation?
I can't get up now.

I'm eighty years old.
I'm too old to get up now.
At least I'm not bald.

Parker Rice (9)
Holme Slack CP School, Preston

Growing Up

Haiku poetry

I'm 13 years old.
I'm officially a teen.
I'm so stressed. Help me!

I'm 20 years old.
I just want money, no kids!
Kids are annoying!

I'm 60 years old.
I've got an injured back and
I wish I were young.

Muhammad-Husayn Shah (9)
Holme Slack CP School, Preston

Fourteen, Twenty, Sixty

I'm fourteen years old.
I like the standing toilet.
I have diarrhoea.

I'm twenty years old.
I failed my hard test.

I'm sixty years old.
My back hurts so much.
I have twenty bad problems.
I need help to walk.

Shehroz Khurram (9)
Holme Slack CP School, Preston

Getting Old

I'm twenty years old
My kids keep slapping me, it hurts
I have a fancy car

I am fifty years old
I have a job and some kids
I have armpit hair

I am sixty years old
I forgot how much sleep I had
My back hurts a lot.

Daniel Mahoney (9)
Holme Slack CP School, Preston

Untitled

Haiku poetry

I am ten years old
My mum calls me a baby
Chicken, banana.

I'm twenty years old
One plus one is three, I'm smart
I am a slay girl.

I'm ninety years old
My grandkids say I am old
I'm Mr Lonely.

Abdul Rehman (9)
Holme Slack CP School, Preston

Untitled

I'm 30 years old.
I ate my cat for lunch.

I'm 60 years old.
If you break your back put a paper towel on it, or ice.

I'm 90 years old.
I hate being old.

Jackson Heap (9)
Holme Slack CP School, Preston

The Death Of Eugene Paul Jr

There once was a child named Eugene Paul Jr,
And he was the nerdiest kid that existed here.
One day, he entered a science competition,
To go and see a replica rocket mission.
The judge saw his entry and really liked it,
So he let him go and see the replica rocket.
On the bus trip, he got so excited,
He opened the window and almost jumped out of it.
When he arrived, the rockets were side by side,
But he couldn't tell the difference, even by size.
The tour guide said to go on the left rocket,
But he was too busy missing his plug socket.
So Eugene thought he said to go to the right,
So Eugene did it without even a fright.
The rocket launched with Eugene on it,
He was confused because the replica didn't do it.
After a while, he found himself on Luna,
"oH mY gOsH, tHIs is So aweSOmE!" said Eugene Paul
Jr.
Eugene started exploring the moon,
When an alien appeared behind him, coloured maroon.
Then the alien ate him and announced, "This is
Glorpshift."

Ben Cooksey (10) & Leo Price (10)
Little Sutton Primary School, Sutton Coldfield

Faith, The Feline Empress

Golden brown with royal grace,
A black-pawed foot, her badge in place.
She struts the hall with lots of pride,
Queen of sass, she doesn't hide.

She claims your lap – but on her terms,
While judging you with subtle squirms.
She rules the room with just one glare,
From a velvet throne that's always there.

Affection's rare, a sacred rite,
A fleeting purr, a sweet invite.
But blink too long or stroke too wide?
She'll toss her tail and shun your side.

Don't be deceived by her purring pace,
She has a plan for every space.
She knocks things down, you still obey –
She's the tiger, you're the prey.

Zac Foster (10) & Brian Jin (10)
Little Sutton Primary School, Sutton Coldfield

What Just Happened?

I went to the park
Then I saw a shark
Then I realised it couldn't move
But in reality, it could use its hoof to move
So I ran away
Then started to play
I started to have fun
But I realised I needed to run!
Then I saw a nail
Trying to be pale
Then I saw a human
Then saw my good friend, Humion
Or so I thought
And I caught him in a cage, but it was Jim!
Then I said sorry to him
Then I saw a flower
And it had lots of power
Then I had anxiety
Then woke up from a dream
And I was mean in my dream
So I was really mad
Then I was sad
Because I had a nightmare.

Adam Truby (10)
Little Sutton Primary School, Sutton Coldfield

Book Boy

There once was a boy who knew everything about
books,
He memorised pictures in them,
Read them multiple times,
Told everyone about them,
Recreated their rhymes,

He read book after book,
Tale after tale,
Picked one up and read it alone,
Taking himself to a land of his own,

There were some about unicorns,
Some about food,
Some about trees,
It was like his eyes were glued,

He would read and read and read and read,
He said it was the only way he felt freed,
He loved it because it would take him somewhere else,
Somewhere he believed in himself.

Harvaani Kaur Bassan (10)
Little Sutton Primary School, Sutton Coldfield

Stardust

Space is a deep, dark hole,
Galaxies and solar systems everywhere,
It's as black and as dark as coal,
With supplies of very little air.

Your imagination takes you to another place,
A place with only you,
With pulsars, quasars, nebulae, white dwarfs,
And a billion things hidden from view.

Does space last forever?
Where does it start? Where does it end?
Will we see the answer,
In the light that gravity bends?

Our place in this vast cosmos,
Explore it we must,
By doing this, we'll find ourselves,
As we are mere stardust.

Isabella Cross (9)
Little Sutton Primary School, Sutton Coldfield

Solar System Trip!

Come aboard, come aboard,
This rocket ship,
Be quick, be quick,
We are leaving Earth,
To go aboard to find out more about our planet mates!
We'll zoom around Saturn,
And Mercury, then Mars,
Observe Venus and see Neptune!
And you'll spot six billion stars!
Jupiter and Uranus!
Pluto! And our planets, stars (the moon),
If not, if not,
There's another day,
Just wait, just wait,
Until the day!

Chloe Bugaj (10)
Little Sutton Primary School, Sutton Coldfield

Summertime

S ummertime is full of fun,
U nder the warmth of the sun.
M elting ice creams, dripping everywhere,
M emories of having fun out there.
E veryone has a smile on their face,
R elaxing in their own sunny space.
T ime with family is best,
I n the sunlight beams to rest.
M ustn't forget to wear suncream!
E specially in these blazing beams.

Katie Crawford (9)
Little Sutton Primary School, Sutton Coldfield

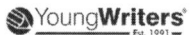

The Trees

Trees shed leaves,
Onto their lumpy knees,
When the leaves fall,
The conkers start to grow,
Grow, grow, grow to a chestnut,
Shed some conkers.
Repeat, repeat, repeat,
And if you want to help,
Just plant, plant, plant!

Michael Welch (10)
Little Sutton Primary School, Sutton Coldfield

Food Philosophy

An apple a day keeps the doctor away!
A banana a night doesn't give you a fright!
If you really care, have a pear!
If you're a girl, eat a Twirl!
If you need aid, have some lemonade!
If you're in a fix, eat a Twix!
If you believe in Santa, have a Fanta!
If you're very far, have a Mars bar!
If you're feeling flat, have a KitKat!
If you're feeling zero, have a miniature hero!
If you're feeling shallow, have a marshmallow!
If you're feeling green, have a tangerine!
If you want to sing a ballad, have a salad!
Put that jelly in your belly!
Eat a candy cane in the rain!
If you're in despair, have a chocolate eclair!
Don't scream, have some ice cream!
Don't cry, have some pie!
Can I have some cheese, please?
If you want to run faster, have some pasta!

Lucie Ward (10)
Shotton Primary School, Shotton Colliery

All About Nature

Have you ever wondered what are all the key details of nature? Well, first, everyone has to know about the waterfalls, don't they? I'll tell you a bit about waterfalls. Waterfalls are any point in a river or stream where water flows over a vertical drop, or a series of steep drops. Waterfalls go splash.

Does everyone know about the flowers? I'll tell you! Flowers are also known as blooms or blossoms. They are the reproductive structures of flowering plants. Typically, they are structured in four circular levels, called whorls, around the end of a stalk.

What about trees, you know about them? If not, I'll tell you. In botany, a tree is a perennial plant with an elongated stem or trunk. Usually supporting branches and leaves. In some usages, the definition of a tree may be narrowed.

Now you know more about nature, here are some quotes about nature.

'In nature, we heal'.

'Nature whispers, listen closely'.

'Wild hearts run free'.

'Mountains are calling, go'.

'Nature nurtures the spirit'.

'Wander often, wander always'.
'Find peace in the wild'.
'Earth's beauty, soul's solace'.

Jasmine Robson (9)

Shotton Primary School, Shotton Colliery

The Wonderverse Disaster

Not very long ago, a young woman called Kate (who worked at Wonderverse Studios) went on a relaxing walk when all of a sudden she saw a beautiful tree (even though it didn't have any leaves or colour). She went to that tree anyway.

Five years later, she revisited the tree, it had colour now and leaves, it had completely changed, a bit too much. There was a little door, then she heard a loud *boom*. The door was open, a big black hand pulled her in. She was really scared, then she found someone. She was called Evelyn.

Kate stayed with Evelyn for a few nights and then she started hearing noises, until she finally opened her eyes. The person who was making her life a living hell was her husband. She was late for work, she was almost fired.

Evelyn Adams (9)
Shotton Primary School, Shotton Colliery

Little Luke The Brave

Luke is three and full of fun,
He laughs and jumps, and loves to run.
He hugs his bear and wears cool shoes,
And sometimes gets his favourite juice.

He has this thing called diabetes,
So he gets checks - yes, even these.
A little poke, a tiny beep,
Then off he goes, no time to sleep.

Though Luke is small, he's big and strong,
He's brave and bright, all day long.
He smiles and plays, he doesn't hide,
With love and courage by his side.

Erin Porter (10)
Shotton Primary School, Shotton Colliery

Growing Up

Growing up, I always had fantastic friends.
They were Mickey, Finn,
Blake, Elijah and Charlie
They were fantastic friends.

I used to have imaginary friends:
Finn, Flinn, Faith and probably others.
I was a fun friend: faithful, and I helped my friends.
That's the story about me growing up with five
fantastic friends.

Harrison Baker (10)
Shotton Primary School, Shotton Colliery

Out Of Space

I wish I was an astronaut
Floating in outer space
Looking down on Planet Earth
While I'm on the moon
Watching the world pass by.

Oh, how I wish I was in outer space
To see all the stars up close
If I could catch a one
I'd bring it back for you.

Nathan Thomas Mace (10)
Shotton Primary School, Shotton Colliery

Nibbles

N ew pet.

I love her with all my heart.

B ig bright eyes.

B rave when she swings from her cage.

L oving when she's handled.

E ats anything, including her cage.

S peedy, running around in her ball.

Katelyn Bright (10)

Shotton Primary School, Shotton Colliery

Growing Up And Living

When you get an English or maths book, you learn
When you learn, you go to college
When you finish college, you get a good job
When you get a good job, your life is complete
So take life one step at a time.

Isabella Evans (10)
Shotton Primary School, Shotton Colliery

Lay On The Summer Day

Oh what a lovely day,
With no dismay,
Lying down on the bay on the sand,
Listening to a band.

Hooray, hooray!
It's truly a special day,
Yay, yay, yay!
For the summer day.

Mikey Greener (10)
Shotton Primary School, Shotton Colliery

The Robber King Of Sounds

Inspired by 'The Sound Collector' by Roger McGough

A stranger came to the woods yesterday,
Dressed in all white and green,
Put all the sounds into a sack,
And he was so, so mean.

The *whooshing* of the air,
The *swishing* of the trees,
The *splashing* of the puddles,
And the *buzzing* of the bees.

The *rattling* of the roundabout,
The *clashing* of the rain,
People slipping over,
They are in so much pain.

The shouting of the people,
The squeaking of the swings,
The squealing of the kids,
As they start to jump off things.

A stranger came to the woods yesterday,
He didn't leave a word,
Left us only silence,
It's the quietest I've heard.

Isabella Toms Gascoigne (8)
Southwick Primary School, Southwick

The Sound Stealer

Inspired by 'The Sound Collector' by Roger McGough

A stranger came to the park today,
Dressed all in purple and white,
Put all the sounds into a bag,
It gave me a big fright.

The laughing of the children,
The squeaking of the slide,
The rattling of the roundabout,
As the children go for a ride.

The stomping of the feet,
The chirping of the birds,
The screaming of children,
Possibly the loudest sound I've heard.

The cheering of the children,
The barking of the dogs,
The bashing of the trees,
The crashing of the logs.

A stranger came to the park today,
He didn't leave a sound,
Left us only silence,
He took everything except the ground.

Bella Stead (8)
Southwick Primary School, Southwick

The School Stalker

Inspired by 'The Sound Collector' by Roger McGough

A stranger came to school in the afternoon,
Dressed in all blue and white,
Put all the sounds into a bag,
It gave me such a fright.

The turning of the key,
The squeaking of the pen,
The talking of the children,
They'd started to shout again.

The talking of the staff,
The scraping of the knife,
The banging of the children,
Running for their life.

The whooshing of the wind,
The squeaking of the slide,
The chirping of the bird,
A child claiming he almost died.

A stranger came to school in the afternoon,
He didn't leave a clue,
Left us only silence,
All he said was, "Boo!"

Effy Richardson (8)
Southwick Primary School, Southwick

The Sound Stalker

Inspired by 'The Sound Collector' by Roger McGough

A stranger came to school yesterday,
Dressed all in grey and white,
He put all the sounds into a bag,
He gave me such a fright.

The banging of the tray,
The yapping of the children,
The chirping of the birds,
As everyone ran into the building.

The flapping of the door,
The sizzling of the sand,
The swishing of the grass,
As everyone plays on the land.

The talking of the teacher,
The flapping of the book,
The laughing of the children,
At how the class clown looks.

A stranger came to school yesterday,
He didn't leave a trace,
He left us with only silence,
I hope he trips on his lace.

Oluwakorede Akinola (8)
Southwick Primary School, Southwick

A Savannah Sound Collector

Inspired by 'The Sound Collector' by Roger McGough

A stranger came to the Savannah last year,
Dressed all in red and green,
Put all the sounds into his luggage,
After that, he was never seen.

The roaring of the lion,
The hissing of the snake,
The puffing of the rhino,
Oh, for goodness' sake.

The crashing of the river,
The whooshing of the snow,
The bubbling of the fish,
The famous penguin I know.

The munching of the adults,
The crunching of the crisps,
The laughing of the people,
When they are eating chips.

A stranger came to the Savannah last year
He didn't leave a sound
Left us only silence
And there was nothing ever found.

Emmanuella Goodness Osho (8)
Southwick Primary School, Southwick

The School Collector

Inspired by 'The Sound Collector' by Roger McGough

A stranger came to school this hour,
Dressed all in black and white,
Put all the sounds into a suitcase,
It gave me such a fright.

The talking of the children,
The slamming of the door,
The bouncing of the ball,
The stomping on the floor.

The whispering of the people,
The clicking of the board,
The crashing of the chair,
The knocking of the door.

The screaming of the children,
The swishing of the trees,
The singing of the birds,
The children asking, "Please?"

A stranger came to school this hour,
He didn't leave a sound,
Left us only silence,
He will never ever be found.

Anthony Ramon Green Martinez (8)
Southwick Primary School, Southwick

The Sound Thief At School

Inspired by 'The Sound Collector' by Roger McGough

A stranger came to school at two o'clock,
Dressed all in yellow and white,
Put all the sounds in a backpack,
He gave me a fright.

The smacking of the trays,
The clicking of the switch,
The bouncing of the ball,
The laughing of the witch.

The meowing of the cat,
The barking of the dog,
The cheeping of the birds,
The knocking of the log.

The clattering of the dinner,
The mocking of the food,
The asking of the chef,
The scraping of the spoon.

A stranger came to school at two o'clock,
He didn't leave a trace,
Left us only silence,
Then left to go to his place.

Oluwkitan David Bakare (8)
Southwick Primary School, Southwick

The Mysterious Guest In The Hotel

Inspired by 'The Sound Collector' by Roger McGough

A stranger checked in this minute,
Dressed all in yellow and green,
Put all the sounds into a case,
And tried not to be seen.

The bubbling of the bathtubs,
The pattering of the sink,
The flushing of the toilet,
So it does not stink.

The squeaking of the curtains,
The clattering of the toys,
The whooshing of the bed sheets,
Making loads of noise.

The snapping of the chocolate,
The laughing of the children,
The munching of the adults,
Inside the massive, blank building.

A stranger checked in this minute,
She didn't leave her shoe,
Why did she take all the sounds?
If only I knew.

Zoe Oghenovo (8)
Southwick Primary School, Southwick

The Creepy Sound Collector At The Zoo!

Inspired by 'The Sound Collector' by Roger McGough

A stranger came to the zoo today,
Dressed all in pink and white,
Put all the sounds into a bag,
I totally got a fright.

The stomping of the elephant,
The hopping of the bunny,
The screaming of the children,
The rumbling of my tummy.

The whirring of the engine,
The clashing of the money,
The slopping of the ice cream
When it all gets runny.

The waddling of the penguins,
The crunching of the ice,
The splashing of the water,
The sound of children being nice.

A stranger came to the zoo today,
She didn't leave a clue,
Left us only silence,
Why, I haven't got a Scooby-Doo.

Lilah June Haddock (8)
Southwick Primary School, Southwick

The Blue And Yellow Collector

Inspired by 'The Sound Collector' by Roger McGough

A stranger came to school yesterday,
Dressed all in yellow and blue,
Put all the sounds into a backpack,
He took everything except my shoe.

The talking of the chefs,
The clashing of the trays,
The squeaking of the scooters,
As the children play.

The scraping of the forks,
The chopping of the food,
The shouting of the children,
When they're in a mood.

The bouncing of the ball,
The squeaking of the slide,
The creaking of the bike,
When the children ride.

A stranger came to school yesterday,
He didn't leave a clue,
Left us only silence,
Now the sky will not be blue.

Nyah-Lee Wright (8)
Southwick Primary School, Southwick

The Day The Visitor Came

Inspired by 'The Sound Collector' by Roger McGough

A visitor came to school in the afternoon,
Dressed all in red and white,
Put all the sounds in a suitcase,
And followed the light.

The scraping of the pen,
The talking of the staff,
The clattering of the tray,
As the children laughed.

The banging of the tables,
The crunching of the food,
The swaying of the blinds,
Because the bad boys moved.

The turning of the key,
The kicking of the feet,
The playing of the music,
The children follow the beat.

The visitor came to school in the afternoon,
He did not leave his name,
Left us only silence,
If only a sound could be found.

Isaac Huggins (7)
Southwick Primary School, Southwick

The Colourful Sound Collector

Inspired by 'The Sound Collector' by Roger McGough

A stranger came to my neighbourhood,
Dressed all in red and blue,
Put all the sounds in a case,
And she never left a clue.

The crying of the children,
The tweeting of the bird,
The swishing of the trees,
The loudest sounds I've heard.

The *whooshing* of the wind,
The barking of the dog,
The gossiping of the neighbour,
The tapping of the log.

The singing of the music.
The skipping of the rope.
The beeping of the cars.
The bubbling of the soap.

A stranger came to my neighbourhood this second.
She didn't leave a sound.
Left us only silence.
She was never ever found.

Mmasinachi Abasirim (7)
Southwick Primary School, Southwick

The Robbery At The Farm

Inspired by 'The Sound Collector' by Roger McGough

A stranger came to the farm today,
Dressed in all red and green,
Put all the sounds into a sack
And that was all I'd seen.

The stomping of the cow,
The oinking of the pig,
The sneezing of the horses
As I started to dig.

The howling of the kids,
The crunching of the crisps,
The pecking of the birds,
The squeaking of the chicks.

The screaming of the children,
The whooshing of the swing,
The banging of the tractors,
The beeping sound it brings.

A stranger came to the farm today,
He didn't leave a sound,
Left us only silence,
Will they ever be found?

Harper Mae Drew Harrison (8)
Southwick Primary School, Southwick

The Day That The Stranger Came To School

Inspired by 'The Sound Collector' by Roger McGough

A stranger came to school yesterday,
Dressed all in green and white,
Put all the sounds into a purse,
And the purse looked so tight.

The slamming of the tray,
The clashing of the cupboard door,
The clicking of the light switch,
The stomping on the floor.

The laughing of the people,
The swishing of the trees,
The bouncing of the ball,
The tapping of the keys.

The stranger came to school yesterday,
He didn't leave his shoe,
He left us only silence,
He must not have had a clue.

Lilly-Rose Harding
Southwick Primary School, Southwick

The Town Monster

Inspired by 'The Sound Collector' by Roger McGough

A stranger came to the town this afternoon
Dressed in purple and blue,
Put all the sounds into a bag
Then even took my shoe.

The talking of the people,
The beeping of the cars,
The singing of the music,
The beating of the hearts.

The stirring of the coffee,
The munching of the food,
The talking of the people,
Everyone was in a good mood.

A stranger came to the town this afternoon,
She didn't leave a single clue
Left us only silence:
Her favourite colour must be blue.

Kanzi Hegazi (8)
Southwick Primary School, Southwick

The Pink Sound Collector

Inspired by 'The Sound Collector' by Roger McGough

A stranger came to school last hour.
Dressed all in red and pink,
Put every sound into a pink bag,
He left in a wink.

The slamming of the table,
The dripping of the tap,
The squeaking of the pens,
The whiteboard on my lap.

The scraping of the knife,
Because someone's in a mood,
The whispering of the people,
The chewing of the food.

A stranger came to school last hour,
He only left this note,
Left us all in silence,
It must have dropped from his coat.

Jenson-James McCririe (8)
Southwick Primary School, Southwick

The Unexpected

I believe in the science of life
I believe in fire, earth and ice
I believe in microscopic little lice
I believe in things I cannot see
I believe in things taught to me
But fairies, no, no, I would never believe it.

Sombre and silent were the woods that day
But all my life, I'd journeyed that way
Ephemeral shadows fluttered around
Like tricks of the eye, it made no sound
Yet today, it was different, eerily ominous
My fear was silent, silent and dolorous.

Then, a silver, shimmering dart
Flew past and startled, startled my heart
Her wings were candescent, lit like a candle
I saw her, a fairy, but this, I couldn't handle
Coming close, her cheeks were blushy-pink
Her eyes beady and bubbly, she gave me a wink.

I wanted more, but then it vanished
And with that, all my beliefs were banished
And now I walk in the enchanted woods
I crave to see what cannot be understood
And if someone says fairies aren't real
Just know in the woods, you can see one for real.

Raphaela Papathanasiou (10)
St Faith's CE Primary School, Wandsworth

The Sunflower

Once there was a sunflower
That was ready to *pop* out of the ground
When that happened...
The sunflower grew and grew and *grew!*
It grew leaves, petals until...
It stopped!

The bees saw the new flower
And took it in turns
To collect the sunflower nectar
And that sunflower is here today
Providing food for the little bees

Its colours illuminate the field
Starry yellow, brunette brown
Once there was a sunflower
That memory makes me smile.

Madison McGowan (9)
St Faith's CE Primary School, Wandsworth

The Rainforest

T he rain always falls on me
H igh up in the air I stare
E choing if someone can see me.

R ain, rain the only thing out there
A frog jumps to a flower like a tower
I wish I had a friend
N ight and light, it's when I sleep
F ight the night, I hear voices
O h no, it's a scary sound
R an far away every day
E very time the rain drips
S ee the rainforest
T he beauty will come.

Savino Hoxha (10)
St Faith's CE Primary School, Wandsworth

Valentine's Day

V alentine's Day is a special day,

A s you wait, you wonder who you are going to go with

L ater, you find the perfect person,

E veryone waits to be your match, but you have already chosen,

N ot everyone can be your match,

T ell your friends the news,

I gnore the rude moments if you get any

N o one can ruin your mood because you are a star and

E veryone is jealous,

S omeone is your valentine and you have the best one.

Nadia Bigovic (9)
St Faith's CE Primary School, Wandsworth

Once I Saw A Butterfly...

Once I saw a butterfly
Soaring up into the Maya blue sky.

Twice I saw a butterfly
Capri-blue wings fluttering so high.

Three times I saw a butterfly!
Then two, three
After that, only a parade could I see.

Some apricot-orange, some honey-yellow
Twirling, twirling
As if they were saying hello!

Once I saw a butterfly
And now...
I'm soon to die
These are my last words to the ecstatic, exultant
butterflies
Goodbye.

Menia Papathanasiou (10)
St Faith's CE Primary School, Wandsworth

Lily And Eelfy The Elf

Eelfy the elf
She is
Pointy ears
Blonde hair
Happy, no tears
Kind and fair
Full of joy
BFF with Lily
Pretty like a toy
Funny and silly

It's me, Eelfy the Elf

Lily the elf
She is
Pointy ears
Brown hair
Filled with cheer
Hairclip, which is spare
Full of joy
BFF with Eelfy
Never annoy
Good at selfies

It's me, Lily the elf.

Anna Chornii (10)
St Faith's CE Primary School, Wandsworth

Smaller

Words are small, they can get *big*
They can get small, like this stupid sentence
Blah, blah, blah, blah 4
Blah, blah, blah 3
Blah, blah 2
Blah 1
0
You see, words get small or *big* like this
Blah, blah, blah
So yes, small/big it's the same like win or lose, win or lose, giant and tiny, you'll never know the difference, large, thin, we will never know the difference.

Cherish Asare (10)
St Faith's CE Primary School, Wandsworth

Gaming Setup

One day, I woke up and asked my dad, "Could I get a gaming setup?"

He said, "Yes."

I was so excited. Then I put my shoes on and we went to the store. When I got it, I started playing Roblox and got some Robux.

I told all my friends and they said, "It's cool. Do you want to play Fortnite with us?"

I said, "Yes."

Kaleb Mensah (10)
St Faith's CE Primary School, Wandsworth

Nature's Fun!

Don't stay inside to age and lay,
When you could go outside and play!
Instead of sitting and watching TV,
You could go on a swing and say *wheee!*
Don't play Fortnite and 1v1,
When you could play with a friend in the sun.
Don't be a Roblox kid and get no chores done,
Go touch some grass and realise nature's fun!

Ameiah Stewart (10)
St Faith's CE Primary School, Wandsworth

Why I Like Space

First, it's as black as some cats
It reminds me of a hat
A rat in a hat
A rocket which brightens the dark
It's so cold outside
As deadly as a fart
The fart is destructive like a dart
And fast enough for a go-kart
And the cat in the hat...
Let's say he's not very smart.

Adem De Ruyter (10)
St Faith's CE Primary School, Wandsworth

The Spaceship

I creep through the halls
I can see a window by the wall
I check through the window
And all I see
Are stars and planets
And they all look the same to me.

It is lonely on the spaceship
I'm going back home to my planet
It was nice knowing you.
Bye.

Blake Causer (10)
St Faith's CE Primary School, Wandsworth

Butterfly

B eautiful wings spread wide
U nique in every way
T ruly magnificent
T winkling through the night
E ver-ending journey
R eally lovely
F lying high as you can
L anding on hand to hand
Y ou are amazing.

Lorelei Hennessy (10)
St Faith's CE Primary School, Wandsworth

Growing Up

First, you're a baby, always crying
Second, you're a toddler, always lying
Third, you're a kid, always playing
Fourth, you're a secondary, always grading
After, you're an adult, paying the bills
Lastly, you're old, acting still.

Kiara De Silva (10)
St Faith's CE Primary School, Wandsworth

History's Past

Haiku poetry

In the depths of time
Revealing the past's secrets
Look into the world.

You can run for now
Time is now an endless void
The past is unknown.

Look at yourself now
It's a cruel reality
It's time to go now.

Waafi Azim (10)
St Faith's CE Primary School, Wandsworth

Hot Sun

H ot like a blazing heater
O h, we need to put our sunscreen on
T he sun gets hotter every day

S o hurry up
U and me need time to play
N ow look, what a beautiful sight it is to see
everybody play.

Anthony Do (10)

St Faith's CE Primary School, Wandsworth

Untitled

I have great friends
I love art so much
I have siblings
My birthday is on June 17th
Purple, pink, red
I love painting and drawing
I love watching videos
I love crafting
I don't like black
I love playing Roblox.

Vanessa Ingabire (9)
St Faith's CE Primary School, Wandsworth

The Best Friendship Ever

Friendship is when you help them when they trip
It is like when you're holding a strip.
They will like the same things like chocolate chip.
They are always in partnership.
They will vote the same thing on a voting slip.

Bareera Iftiklar (10)
St Faith's CE Primary School, Wandsworth

The Sonic Poem

Inside of Green Hills
Golden rings are piled up
With Chaos Emeralds too
The hedgehog speeds around at ease
It is just a quiet day
And nothing can go wrong...

Finley Woolford (10)
St Faith's CE Primary School, Wandsworth

Hidden Histories

Haiku poetry

The past is hidden
A history of secrets
In the depths alone

Unknown history
Hidden in the void, not found
Where no one can find.

Reuben Balcombe (10)
St Faith's CE Primary School, Wandsworth

A Penguin's Journey

Inside an egg, a gentle scratch,
A tiny beak begins to hatch,
Out comes a chick all soft and grey,
Much too small to catch its own prey,
So Mum goes out hunting in the storm,
While the chick snuggles up to Dad to keep warm.

All grown up, now look at what she's become,
White belly, yellow beak, a tall adult mum,
Thick, black, oily feathers to dry off after racing to the water,
She needs to get food for her nearly-hatched daughter,
Webbed feet to kick through the sea,
One fish, two, now, finally, three,
Just enough for the whole family.

As she climbs out, she sees a blanket of white,
The snow and ice making a magnificent sight,
Strong, persistent winds roaring across the Antarctic sky,
Across mountains that are exceedingly high,
Waddling home to have her snack,
She sees her egg begin to crack!

Inside the egg a gentle scratch,
A tiny beak begins to hatch,
Out comes a chick all soft and grey,
Much too small to catch its own prey,
So Mum gives it food that she just caught,
Looking back, *what a wonderful life I've had,* she
thought.

Miriam Hunt (11)
St Thomas' Catholic Primary School, Sevenoaks

Rocky The Rockhopper

Rocky was a penguin who started up north,
His need to change, to move down south, brought
evolution forth.
Slow as it happened, nonetheless,
To help him swim and catch his prey,
To keep his species fresh.

Up came his hair to little tight spikes,
Add some yellow streaks to that,
And his hairstyle you might like.
Threatened as they are, to being vulnerable,
They find a way to survive the day,
By changing how they feed.

Mainly in the Falklands, the southern species thrives,
They may be small, but hardy,
They are to elongate their lives.
Evolving is essential to give species life,
They must evolve to keep themselves strong,
And help them all survive.

Swimming in cold waters,
The feathers are locked in nice,
They keep them warm and waterproof,
And keep them safe from ice.
Hoping that they continue to win the survival fight,
They may be small, but tough enough,
To survive another night.

Mason Vollings (11)
St Thomas' Catholic Primary School, Sevenoaks

One Creature, Two Varying Worlds

Skill, survival, sustenance, all the lioness needs,
Patrolling her grounds,
Preparing to pounce,
Scouts the danger,
Protects her life,
Camouflages in the tawny, desiccated savannah,
Long retractable claws tighten,
Ready for a full-force spectacle,
Limitless withdrawal,
The leaps vibrating with agility,
Seeing with force,
Teeth dig.

Separated by sea,
Bound in a forest, but free,
Dying, crying, weeping, 600 remain,
Head wrapped in sparse mane,
Through the forest I stalk.
Claws gripped the ground,
Prepared for any sound,

Stealthy as a beautiful steed,
I have my own selective needs,
A difference in environment,
African and Asian,
Each unique and special,
Can learn to thrive in plains and forest.

Anita Bagchee (10)
St Thomas' Catholic Primary School, Sevenoaks

My Blue Butterfly

I watched a beautiful blue butterfly,
Its opalescent wings, like the pages of a book,
Flicking through all the seasons,
Waiting to see what the next chapter of life brings.

In a glorious garden under the scorching sun,
She nested on a flower while feeding on its nectar,
Surely the butterflies would be safe there,
That's what I thought, until the birds came by.

A wave of butterflies fled the garden,
Leaving the nest to camouflage there,
In flowers and under leaves,
Wherever their colourful wings could hide them.

When the greedy birds had grown full,
And flew on away into the twilight sky,
Most of the butterflies come out from hiding,
Except my blue butterfly, who had faced her fate.

Alexa Wyss (11)
St Thomas' Catholic Primary School, Sevenoaks

The Arctic Fox

As winter rolls by, you turn white,
You nest in your snowy den at night
Keeping out of sight.

Hiding from the polar bear,
You dash as you see it near.
You keep your soft kits out of harm's way,
So the fluffy snowflakes can live another day.

Buds appear from under the bitter snow,
While verbenas hang low,
And the sun makes you glow.

Your kits leave,
As you are left alone to grieve,
You find shelter from the boiling sun,
All the other animals have fun.

The breeze starts to come back,
Your fur starts to change from black,
Your prey starts to slack.
Another winter rolls by, and you turn white once more.

Nina Grahovac (11)
St Thomas' Catholic Primary School, Sevenoaks

The Polar Bear

Out in the frozen land,
Silence fills the air,
Its massive paws like boots,
Keeps her up on slick ice.

Her cloak as white as a ghost,
Hides her Arctic frost,
But under her pure robe,
Black skin sucks in the sunlight.

With lungs of steel the polar bear swims through the
bitter sea,
She glides for miles in the numbing breeze,
Paddling through the freezing ocean,
She looks for her next prey to take down.

With dark, cunning eyes,
With a strong nose,
She senses her next victim
And eats with no hesitation.

Out in the frozen land,
Silence fills the air,
Far in the harsh Arctic,
Lives the polar bear.

Natalia Dziedzic (10)
St Thomas' Catholic Primary School, Sevenoaks

Penguin

Splish, splash, splosh, the penguins dive in,
To grab the frightened fish.
They protect their skin from getting wet,
When they hunt for their dish.
A thick layer of fat to keep them warm,
When they gather together,
It's as crowded as when bees swarm.

The ocean is their shopping store,
With food to eat and lots more.
Another layer of feathers to trap in heat,
When they hunt for food to eat.

In and out and in and out they come from the water,
With sea creatures galore,
Which they've slaughtered.
Penguins are incredible creatures,
With extraordinary, outstanding features.

Alessia Ditri (11)
St Thomas' Catholic Primary School, Sevenoaks

The Sloth

Melting into lush canopies,
Green algae growing on his coarse coat,
Living high in the trees,
Lazily watching the world go by,
Black rings circle earthy brown eyes,
Yet the sloth struggles to see,
Sleeping all day, eating all night.

Effortlessly, the sloth clings onto branches,
Strong curved claws helping him climb,
Hanging like a hammock in a soft seaside breeze,
Moving so slow, no predator can spot him,
Thick, sticky tongue tearing leaves,
An excellent swimmer, paddling to his next adventure,
Sleeping all day, eating all night.

Rebecca Henson (11)
St Thomas' Catholic Primary School, Sevenoaks

My Life As A Capybara

I relax underneath the sun,
My brown fur is coarse and sparse,
To help me blend into the dry grass.
Swimming, swimming into the lake,
Eating fruit and grass for my own sake,
I use my web-shaped feet to glide and swim.
I use my long teeth to rip off grass
And eat more fruit.
I am also very social with my mates around.
I'm the friendliest animal on the ground!
Oh, no! Oh, no!
Here comes a jaguar!
But don't worry - I've got my superpower:
I sink into the lake
Or blend into the grass
So we're all safe and sound!

Nadia Saenz Gonzalez (11)
St Thomas' Catholic Primary School, Sevenoaks

The Fennec Fox

The fennec fox's ears are like fans,
Cooling itself off in the hot air,
Its beige fur, camouflaged in the scorching sand,
Waiting for prey to come near.

The fennec fox's coat is like glass,
Reflecting the sunlight off its body,
His fleece protecting him from the cold nightly breeze,
As well as disguising himself.

The fennec fox's fur is like sandals,
Guarding its feet from the burning, scorching and
dangerous sand,
His waterless kidneys adapting to the waterless
environment,
Never needing to drink again.

Oscar Grabowski (10)
St Thomas' Catholic Primary School, Sevenoaks

The Arctic Fox

In the ice-cold tundra,
The Arctic fox roams,
Its coat, pure white,
Blending into the snow.

Its small, short legs,
Its coat of grace,
Its bushy tail,
Helps the fox to survive the cold, harsh space.

Its black nose,
Sniffing for prey,
Its round ears pricked up,
Listening for danger in its way.

At summertime, soil forms,
The sun shines bright,
The Arctic fox claims a disguise of blue and grey,
Shedding its beautiful coat of snow white.

Caroline Tse (11)
St Thomas' Catholic Primary School, Sevenoaks

Freedom

A pure white dove soars across the dark sky,
I reach out, but it's miles away,
Colourful lights illuminate the city,
Brightening the lonely twilight,
Heavy water droplets seep from grey clouds,
Spattering onto the dusty ground.

I slowly trudge to the dirty shelter,
Wishing I were anywhere else,
Guards usher me inside, locking the door,
My sister sleeps, hiding in dreams,
One day we will be free, as free as a dove.

Anamaria Ford (11)
St Thomas' Catholic Primary School, Sevenoaks

The Dolphin

Splashing in the waves,
Splashing in the water,
The dolphins swim in the world's seas,
Adapting, reducing blood flow in freezing
temperatures,
Whistling, clicking and communicating with each other,
Dolphins swim down by the sea floor, down deep,
Millions of dolphins in our world's seas bring joy when
seen,
Holding their breath for long, adapting to the water,
The sweet sound of them chattering fills the air.

Nikola Wolanin (10)
St Thomas' Catholic Primary School, Sevenoaks

Polar Bear Evolution

Polar bear fur is as white as snow,
A brown bear's fur is as brown as chocolate.
Both bears camouflage themselves in their
surroundings.

My paws once pounded the hard ground.
Now they crunch the icy snow.
Once chasing my prey in the wilderness,
Now I glide along the hard ice.
Once a small, feeble and gentle dog,
Now a fierce monster on the ice.

I wonder what I'll be next?

William Durcan (11)
St Thomas' Catholic Primary School, Sevenoaks

The Glorious Swan

Upon the lake of blue glass,
The place where breezes pass,
A creature glides with grace,
With a glorious white masked face.

The sun beams high in the sky,
Where the beautiful creature lies,
Her feathers are white,
Glistening in the bright light.

The elegance is so still,
Which is full of skill,
But yet, in her eyes,
Within, a storm still cries.

Derin Yalman (11)
St Thomas' Catholic Primary School, Sevenoaks

The Fennec Fox

Quickly, quietly,
Alert to any movement,
The fennec fox stalks,
Silent as a shadow,
She gazes around the sandy Sahara,
She lowers her head,
The fox is in search of her next meal,
Dark clouds cover the sky,
Evening rolls away into a starless night,
Now is the time to hunt,
Running smoothly over the sand,
She senses prey,
The fox makes her kill.

Celestine Disant (11)
St Thomas' Catholic Primary School, Sevenoaks

The Creature Of The Night

The owl is the creature of the night,
It rests all day, but at night it hunts for prey.

Silently, it darts towards its prey,
All ready to slay.

Day after day, it hunts to feed its children.

It carefully looks out for food, checking every millimetre,
So its children won't have to starve.

The owl is the creature of the night.

Andrii Musiyenko (11)
St Thomas' Catholic Primary School, Sevenoaks

I Am A Tiger

I am a tiger, orange and black,
I am a tiger with my streak,
I am a tiger, I pounce on my prey.

I am a tiger, camouflaged but tall,
I am a tiger, effortlessly strong,
I am a tiger, hear my roar.

I am a tiger, large, powerful paws,
I am a tiger, watch me hunt,
I am a tiger, fierce and mighty.

I am a *tiger!*

Aiyla Longworth (10)
St Thomas' Catholic Primary School, Sevenoaks

Untitled No.1

P addle-like wings, otherwise useless on land
E ffortlessly slice through the water
N ot staying out in the cold air alone
G athering together to stay warm
U nderneath their feathers, a layer of blubber
I nsulating their bodies
N ature's brilliant creation.

Alex Sylvester (11)
St Thomas' Catholic Primary School, Sevenoaks

Toca Boca

Have you ever imagined creating your own Wonderverse?

Toca Boca is a mini game of Sims for children!

You can build houses and, even better, people!

But you have to buy houses.

At first you get a mini house and a flat for free!

You even get a lot of shops for free,

A junkyard, theatre, ships and the flat is in it.

The flat is a tall building, but one flat. It's only got one bed though.

You can do what you want whenever you want, but obviously not at school.

There is so much to do! I always play it! It's so much fun!

So much fun! I love it *so much!*

Orlaith Tobin (8)
The Galfrid School, Cambridge

The Strange Planets

Once upon a time, I went to space,
To explore all over the place!
Jupiter, Saturn, Neptune and Mars.
One day, I decided to go to the moon,
I started packing all my favourite snacks.
I got my spacesuit, white and pink,
And off I went to the moon.
When I went, I saw electrical stars, magical storms and flashing lights.

Mariam Amin (8)
The Galfrid School, Cambridge

How Do I Feel?

I play with my friend
Every day, week
Month and year.

I go outside to
Play football and
Basketball every day.
Because I like it.

I play digging with
My friends, playing
Chicken jockey outside.

I'm happy to
Have my family
By my side.

Leonel Sula (9)
The Galfrid School, Cambridge

A Weird Box In Space!

Deep in space, I see a weird box.
This weird box has something inside.
What is the thing inside?
The thing might be a telescope.

What if it is a telescope?
A telescope would be intergalactic.
Intergalactic things are amazing.
Amazing things are exciting and fun.

Sara Islam (8)
The Galfrid School, Cambridge

Space Travel

A wondrous place in space,
You float like a floaty on the water,
You can lie down like you're lying on the bed!
It's as beautiful as the stars!
Imagine your bed; it's comfy!
You see the stars floating towards you!
You feel it. It's bright, soft.

Yumi Distura (8)
The Galfrid School, Cambridge

Emotion Riddle

I snore and snooze
My eyes are closed
I am in my bed
With my covers
Snuggling tight
Fast asleep
Which emotion am I?
One clue
I am sleeping in my bed
That's right
I am sleeping.

Oliver Dutton (7)
The Galfrid School, Cambridge

Animals

A nimals are things
N ot like us
I n the wild
M ad tiger
A ngry roars
L ives flashing
S oon dead.

Teddy Czlonka (8)
The Galfrid School, Cambridge

Space

In space, you can't race
You can't tie your lace
One thing you can do
Is float like you're in the moat.

Kulsoom Wahid (8)
The Galfrid School, Cambridge

Girls' Friendship

Me and my friend Adel
We went to play one day
We decided to go to the beach
To play in the sand and the sea.

Amy Mukaro (8)
The Galfrid School, Cambridge

Roblox Games

Roblox is a place for all
You can play Blade Ball
Zombies die in dead rails
Victory falls like it hails.

Leonardo Pugliese (8)
The Galfrid School, Cambridge

Friendship

The sun is bright
The sky is blue
Friendship everywhere
For me and you.

Sophia El Hassani (7)
The Galfrid School, Cambridge

The Silent Trap

All the forest was as dark as night.
Only the glowing moon was my bright light.
Not even the tiniest spark seen by the human eye.
I was lost, I can't lie.

My only dear friend to comfort me,
Was the cold, bitter winter breeze.
I looked curiously around, up, down, just to see,
The unwelcoming, tall, bare and towering trees.

I lowered my head and heard a single twig snap,
It broke the deafening silence,
And I suddenly realised
I'd been hauled into a trap.

That's when it hit me,
There was no turning back.
Somebody had been following my track.

I was running, I didn't know where
My instinct told me
Someone was giving me a cold, hard death stare.

A sharp, dry laugh sliced the night,
I froze mid-step, gripped by fright.

Ava Brown (10)
Wayfield Primary School, Chatham

Special Things

Everyone has a moment in life where they find a special thing,

You know, something that they're good at like swinging a bat or designing a hat, or even being an acrobat!

Is your mind racing now? Of all the stuff you can do, come on, tell me what makes you zing?

First let me tell you about me and my weird but great family. Don't be freaked out, trust me, good friend, you'll get used to them gradually.

So, first there's my dad and he's a bit mad, very funny, caring, he's the best. He's a big football fan, plays games, drives a van and always wants to rest.

Now there's my mum, she's so fun, you can notice her when she enters the room. She cooks, reads books and has a crazy obsession with perfume!

Next, is my little sister, so innocent and sweet.
But if you put on any music she will surprise you and dance to any beat!

I guess you want to know about me. Well, I love the arts and I also have the smarts to be anything I want to be.

So, with that being said, I can now tell you what really makes me zing.
It's in my heart and in my soul, I will make it you know, I just really love to sing.

So now dear friend, you've heard about us, so tell what's your special thing?

Skylar-Bleu Scott-McKeever (10)
Wayfield Primary School, Chatham

Amazing Animals

Tiger, tiger, orange and black,
Upon his back, fierce and loving,
That's what people love,

When he grows sharp teeth I see,
Sharp and pointy, along his meat,
About night-time, the owls wake up - twitter, twitter,

The owls screech, flying from tree to tree,
Seeing the sun rise, they hide,
Zebra, zebra, black and white,

Early morning, dark of night,
Hunting for food, beware of lion's bite,
Run, run, there might be a way, a way out of sight,

A bunny for a prey,
Bunny, bunny, little ears floppy,
Hop, hop zebra, coming to hide in a hut,
A lion hops, hops away from sight, and sleeps tight,

Lion, king of the jungle,
Other animals have fear,
He is a king with no crown and hates snakes,
Wiggy and sneaky, they come and bite you any second,
Even if you accidentally step on the tail, you will
immediately get bitten,

And contain venom,
Poor animals, night-time has begun,
Sleep tight, stars twinkle as bright they see,

Sharon Adetula (10)
Wayfield Primary School, Chatham

It's Okay Not To Be Okay

Life can feel like juggling,
Throwing things into the air,
Trying hard to catch them,
Trying hard not to be scared.

But know that if you drop one of them,
Things will be okay,
Just pick it up and try again,
Tomorrow's a brand-new day.

When I pause and have a listen,
To what's going on in my mind,
There are some of my thoughts,
That I'd rather leave behind.

I wish I could talk to my worry,
And tell it to go far, far away,
But then I remember I'm human,
So it's okay not to be okay.

Try to talk about your feelings,
To someone that you trust,
Let it out, don't bottle it up,
Talking is a must.

But remember, it's okay not to be okay!

Molly Banham (9)
Wayfield Primary School, Chatham

A Dream

You drift away into a dream where your imagination can take control. When you wake up with all your energy you have so much fun you forget your dream. As you use your energy you get sleepy, so you go to bed and your cat jumps up and starts purring. (You drift away to the purring.) You wake up with not a lot of energy, you are so tired you can't be bothered to do anything, but you remember your dream. So, you start running around trying to tell everyone but your legs start to hurt, so you sit down and wonder how you remember your dream and yesterday you couldn't. Then, you realise today you don't have much energy, so your mind is not as concentrated as yesterday.

Lacie Davies (10)
Wayfield Primary School, Chatham

The Thread Between Us

There is no rhythm to how it starts -
A glance, a shared laugh across a crowded room,
The quiet understanding that says you don't have to
explain yourself here.

Friendship is a thread,
Sometimes invisible,
But strong enough to pull us
Through the noise,
Through the long silences,
Through storms we don't name aloud.

It holds when words falter,
When life turns jagged,
When joy is too big to carry alone.
It stretches - never breaks -
Even across time zones,
Even across seasons of not knowing
Who we are becoming,
We don't always walk side by side,
But your echo is in my steps,
And mine in yours.

That's what friendship is -
Not a promise,
But a presence.

Yensi Kwalar (9)
Wayfield Primary School, Chatham

Friendship And Dislike

Roses are red, violets are blue,
Sugarcane is like my love for you.
You're up high in the sky,
Your eye met mine in the fly
Love is like magic, but for me, it's cruel,
Friends can be nice, even if they're real.
They'll love you until you wilt.
I'll sugar you if you're my friend.

Roses are red, violets are blue,
Lava is like my dislike for you.
You're so low I could not see you,
Me and you did not meet because our eyes did not meet.
Enemies can be nice even if they're real,
Just know they won't be there at the end.
I'll always be there at the mend.

Oreoluwa Ajayi (8)
Wayfield Primary School, Chatham

Why My Home?

I was trotting along
Like a leaf on a windy day
Just like all foxes
But hearing chainsaws and bangs
I paused in my path.

Multiple trees lay lifeless on the path
My home getting destroyed
Nowhere to go
The destructive metal giants were the enemy
It was a constant reminder that my home
Didn't belong to me anymore
Or did it ever?

As if I was an ancient Greek statue,
I stood frozen on display
Anxious and heartbroken
Nowhere to hide and nowhere to feel safe
Humans had demolished my home,
I loved my home and now it was wrecked.

Darcey Thomas (10)
Wayfield Primary School, Chatham

Winter Animals

The snow falls from the sky.
The animals rush to hide.
Snowflakes sparkle and glisten.
The sun has gone down, and the moon has risen.
The snow makes a white, fluffy carpet on the ground.
It's all so beautiful, no one makes a sound.
The animals are safe, warm in their bed.
And with lots of food in their bellies are fed.
So sleep tight animals and get some rest
Winter animals are the best.

Daisy Eldridge (9)
Wayfield Primary School, Chatham

My Dog

My dog was born on a hot summer's day in June,
We gave him a bath, turns out he's a loon,
But that's okay because I love him to the moon.
We call him Bandito, his favourite food is mashed potato.
He is four years old and never does what he's told.
Black and white fur with a face like a rascal.
But what more could you ask, my dog is up to the task!

Summer Passcall (10)
Wayfield Primary School, Chatham

Silly Zebras

I went to the zoo and what did I see?
A herd of zebras watching me.
I moved to the left and then to the right
Jumped up and down and gave them a fright.
They ran away as fast as they could
And ended up getting lost in the wood.
I started dancing and what did I see?
The zebras running back to me.
They went to the shed
And then went to bed.

Louise Robertson (8)
Wayfield Primary School, Chatham

Untitled

The majestic cat, black as night, creeps around timidly
Hides under the sofa, jumps out and bites your feet
Climbs the curtains, attacks the binds
Curled up, he sleeps all day,
Twitching whilst he dreams of his day's adventures
Escapes from the back door and hides in the grass
He is an adorable, adventurous cat.

Sadie Rae Stevens (10)
Wayfield Primary School, Chatham

Untitled

H eroes are good-looking and they read lots of books

E ven though they have mighty fists, that are myths

R eally kind, but have to say goodbye to millions of villains

O n time, every time

E yes that can see all the way to the Atlantic. See with bees

S uperheroes always save the day.

Teddie Lycett (8)
Wayfield Primary School, Chatham

The Weather And Me

Thunder and lightning,
For me can be frightening.
As the rain pours down,
I sit with a frown.
A gust of wind down the street,
I feel unsteady on my feet.
When the snow is settling on the ground,
I sit silently, not making a sound.
But when the sun is in the sky,
It makes me feel like I can fly.

Poppy Yeates (10)
Wayfield Primary School, Chatham

Staying Young, Still BFFs

Inside the human heart, love is above
Friends forever and ever, even when we grow old
But we are still pieces of gold
That will never change, sitting on a hill
Looking at a mill together
When we are not blue we go to the beach too
We love May which is summer and I hope it can stay.

Melody Ovbigbaghon (9)
Wayfield Primary School, Chatham

Christmas

The Christmas tree has glowing lights on it,
It makes me feel like it's Christmas soon,
It brings joy to me,
When it stands proud in winter,
It's like the sun's glow,
In my house it glows,
Every time I run, its lights come on.

Iona Patrick-Ononye (8)
Wayfield Primary School, Chatham

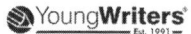

Haunted House

There was a haunted house
With a little brown mouse
Creeping around, making the floorboard creak
With the sound of a squeak
The mouse was weak
And the weather outside was ever so bleak
As the brown little mouse drifted to sleep.

Darcy Fuller (8)
Wayfield Primary School, Chatham

Secrets Of The Crystal Snow

Crystals shine and diamonds are divine,
They shine in the moonlight and twinkle in the twilight sky.
A magical creature lies beyond the snowy forest.
She has fur as soft as snow,
And her name is Snowflake.

Deekshitha Dhibin (8)
Wayfield Primary School, Chatham

Best Friends Forever

So nice to have a friend like you,
Somehow, when you're around,
The sky turns from grey to blue,
The way we can trust each other,
The way we depend on one another.

Poppy Groves (9)
Wayfield Primary School, Chatham

Night

As the sun begins to fall
The animals begin to crawl
As the moon shines
People dine
As the stars sparkle
The water twinkles in the moonlight.

Teddie Beaumont (9)
Wayfield Primary School, Chatham

A Hero

H ero protects our country
E xcellent role model
R esponsible for keeping our country safe
O ne of a kind.

Gorav Adit Donthuiapoina (8)

Wayfield Primary School, Chatham

YOUNG WRITERS INFORMATION

We hope you have enjoyed reading this book – and that you will continue to in the coming years.

If you're the parent or family member of an enthusiastic poet or story writer, do visit our website **www.youngwriters.co.uk/subscribe** and sign up to receive news, competitions, writing challenges and tips, activities and much, much more! There's lots to keep budding writers motivated!

If you would like to order further copies of this book, or any of our other titles, then please give us a call or order via your online account.

Young Writers
Remus House
Coltsfoot Drive
Peterborough
PE2 9BF
(01733) 890066
info@youngwriters.co.uk

Join in the conversation!
Tips, news, giveaways and much more!

 YoungWritersUK   **YoungWritersCW**
 youngwriterscw   **youngwriterscw**

Scan to watch the video!